Apple of His Eye

SETTING YOUR AFFECTIONS ON THINGS ABOVE...

Betty Huizenga

An Apples of Gold Ministries Book

For Orletta

Thank you for giving
a young friend and new neighbor
a hunger for the Word of God
by opening your home and heart
for the purpose of worshiping God
through study and prayer

For the Word of God is living and active.......
Hebrews 4:12

Contents

PART ONE: Getting Started

Introduction 5

Lesson One: Finding Quiet For Your Heart 9

Lesson Two: Listen UP 17

Lesson Three: Learning to Hear God's Whisper 23

Lesson Four: A Heart Issue 33

PART TWO: Results and Benefits of Listening to God

Lesson Five: Communion in God's Word 37

Lesson Six: Finding Time for Study 41

Lesson Seven: A Mind that Seeks Wisdom 45

Lesson Eight: A Gentle Spirit 51

Lesson Nine: A Peaceful Spirit 55

Lesson Ten: A Joyful Spirit 61

PART THREE: Quiet Time with God
Practicing the Presence of Jesus Daily 65

EPILOGUE: Teaching Your Children to Worship 69

PART ONE: Getting Started

Apple of His Eye

SETTING YOUR AFFECTIONS ON THINGS ABOVE (Col.3:2)

Betty Huizenga
Copyright 2007

Introduction
Apple of His Eye

Listening to God! What does that mean to you? Can you really hear His voice? How do we know what the Lord is trying to teach us? We will explore this subject in this book. Learning to listen to God in the stillness of your quiet time will become essential to your growth as a believer. Listening and obeying go hand in hand. Obeying just one of the things God speaks into your heart can change your life. IT CHANGED MY LIFE.

Ephesians 2:10 tells us, "We are God's workmanship, created in Christ Jesus to do good works, which God prepared in advance for us to do." My life from childhood to 1995 was all preparation for the work God planned for me, Apples of Gold. God prepared me not only through my family life, my schooling, my friendships, but through my mistakes and sins. He kept drawing me closer to His side until I was quiet enough to listen to His whisper on the mountains of West Virginia. Ephesians 2:10 is not just for me to claim, but for you as well. After we have heard, we have a choice to make; whether or not we will obey.

Often, women tell me, "I know I must have a quiet time, I need time to pray and study, but I am just not sure how to start a routine that I can follow each day." Each of us has a heart need to pray. Most of us DO pray. Even non-believers pray at times of need. Something within us draws us into prayer when we are sick or needy or afraid.

Some of us pray about everything, others only pray about pressing concerns or needs. True prayer goes hand in hand with faith. Do we believe God can or will do what we pray about?

In 1969, the Lord moved us from the comfort of our hometown to Annapolis, MD. On moving day we were welcomed to the neighborhood by Orletta Gillikin, a Christian neighbor. She welcomed us to the community, and invited me to attend Bible study in her home. Being new in town, I would have gone almost anywhere, but God had a much deeper plan for this friendship.

In Orletta' study and through the church she recommended for us to attend, we grew stronger in our faith and grew hungry to know the Lord more personally. Through Bible study, prayer and worship, our lives were dramatically changed.

God uses His Word to teach us, but He also uses people. He has prepared me for "such a time as this" through precious friends who love Him.

For we are God's workmanship, created in Christ Jesus to do good works, which God prepared in advance for us to do. Ephesians 2:10

It is my prayer for you that by the time you finish reading and studying this book, you will know how to spend time with the Lord, to learn from His Word through the Holy Spirit, bring the desires of your heart to Him, and then learn to "Be still and know that He is God." (Psalm 46:10). Listening to God in prayer will strengthen your life and give you direction. I pray that this time becomes one of the desires of your heart.

The Lord may ask things of you that you are sure you cannot do. He may ask you to serve in a way you are not comfortable, or witness to a friend. But when you are sure you have heard His voice speaking to you through His Spirit, you will be strengthened in your heart and have confidence that the Lord will do it through you. Philippians 4:13 tells us that we can do all things through Him who gives us strength. That includes finding time for time alone with God.

Your Heavenly Father desires time with you even though He already knows all about you and knows the need you have. <u>Take time right now to read Psalm 139</u>. You may have read it many times before, but now read it in the context of fellowship with Him. You will learn that even though He knows absolutely everything about you, He still wants fellowship with you because He created you and loves you.

Have you ever told someone you love that they are the apple of your eye? I desire to be the apple of the Heavenly Father's eye, don't you? That happens when we get to know Him as He knows us. Communion, fellowship, listening with a quiet spirit, and obeying Him will take us to that place of closeness to God.

This book is filled with scripture passages. It is the Word of God that is truly important. It is my prayer for you that you will read carefully all the verses in this book, but more than that, you will seek to go deeper by searching out verses for your life in your own Bible. God's Word has the answers for all the questions of today, and is filled with promises, encouragement and hope. The Bible is a current book, covering every topic we face in the world today.

There are many wonderful books about prayer. This is the one the Lord has put in my heart for you. As He has been teaching me to listen, as I learn the joys of that listening, I long for you to learn to listen as well. The blessings are abundant!

Ephesians 3:14-21

For this reason I kneel before the Father, from whom his whole family in heaven and earth derives its name. I pray that out of his glorious riches he may strengthen you with power through his Spirit in your inner being, so that Christ may dwell in your hearts through faith. And I pray that you, being rooted and established in love, may have power, together with all the saints, to grasp how wide and long and high and deep is the love of Christ, and to know this love that surpasses knowledge – that you may be filled to the measure of all the fullness of God.

Now to him who is able to do IMMEASURABLY MORE than all we ASK or IMAGINE, according to his power that is at work within us, to Him be glory in the church and in Christ Jesus throughout all generations, for ever and ever! AMEN.

Lesson One
Finding Quiet for Your Heart

To study the Word, you will need tools.
You will need a Bible, your own Bible. You will want to mark special passages and make notes. Have a notepad, or better yet, a journal, and pencils at hand. Have in hand your favorite hymn book or book of praise and worship music. This will be a very important part of your time with God.

You should make a special place to meet with the Lord each day. Purchase a good Concordance to look up references.

ARE YOU READY?
The Lord is waiting for you.

REMEMBER
READ – WRITE – APPLY – MEMORIZE

Show the wonder of your great love, you who save by your right hand those who take refuge in you from their foes. Keep me as the apple of your eye: hide me in the shadow of your wings...
Psalm 17:7-9

The Psalmist is asking the Lord to show His love by granting him safety and protection under the shadow of His wings. It reminds me of favorite hymns: Jesus, Draw Me Close, Under His Wings, Nearer, Still Nearer and others.

Write another verse that tells how God protects us.

_____
_____
_____
_____

What hymns or choruses remind you of the protection of the Lord over you?

_____
_____
_____
_____

Sing one or two of them in worship to Jesus as you prepare to listen to Him as He speaks to you through His Spirit.

What a comfort it is to be under the very shadow of the Almighty, to know that He cares so much about us. I believe, in return we are to show great thankfulness to Him. We do that by spending time with Him in prayer and by studying His Word. He seeks a relationship with us, a daily, not to miss time.

When we love someone, time spent together is a treasure. There never seems to be enough time. We just cannot wait to see our husband and children. If they are away for several days, we miss them. When we don't talk with our Heavenly Father for a few days, He, too, misses fellowship with His children. We wouldn't dream of spending days with our family without speaking to them (there should not be, at least). Why, then do we sometimes struggle to find time alone with Him, the Savior of our souls, the One who loves us most, the One we love most?

The more we learn about the Lord from His Word and the more time we spend in prayer, the more we will guard that precious time and not let anything or anyone rob us of it.

If you do not have the desire to study the Word and spend time in prayer, ask the Lord to give you that desire and motivation. The Bible is our guide to life, a road map to guide us.

1) IT IS INSPIRED
   II Timothy 3:16-17
   All scripture is God-breathed and is useful for teaching, rebuking, correcting and training in righteousness.

2) IT IS OUR GUIDE
   Psalm 119:103-105:
   How sweet are your words to my taste, sweeter than honey to my mouth! I gain understanding from your precepts; therefore I hate every wrong path. Your Word is a lamp to my feet and a light to my path

3) IT IS THE WAY TO TRUTH AND MEANING
   John 14:6
   Jesus answered, "I am the way and the truth and the life. No one comes to the Father except through me."

4) IT IS THE PATH TO PROTECTION
   Psalm 121:5-8
   The Lord watches over you-the Lord is your shade at your right hand; the sun will not harm you by day, nor the moon by night. The Lord will keep you from all harm – he will watch over your life; The Lord will watch over your coming and going both now and evermore.

James 1:19-25.
My dear brothers, take note of this: Everyone should be quick to listen, slow to speak and slow to become angry, for man's anger does not bring about the righteous life that God desires. Therefore, get rid of all moral filth and the evil that is so prevalent and humbly accept the word planted in you, which can save you.

Do not merely listen to the word, and so deceive yourselves. DO WHAT IT SAYS. Anyone who listens to the word but does not do what it says is like a man who looks at this face in a mirror and, after looking at himself, goes away and immediately forgets what he looks like. But the man who looks intently into the perfect law that gives freedom, and continues to do this, not forgetting what he has heard, but doing it – he will be blessed in what he does.

Write in your own words how you can apply this scripture to your life.

_____

_____

_____

As you to seek His Word, explore your concordance, and ask the Holy Spirit to teach you. Spend that time with the Lord in orderly, meaningful, daily and practical ways. Ask the Lord to make plain the things that are hard to understand, thank Him for the revelations He does give to you. Choose to put into practice the things you are being taught. Your hunger for the Word will increase in unexpected ways, your spiritual growth will bring joy and peace to your life.

Paraphrase Matthew 5:48 in your own words:

Be perfect, therefore, as our heavenly Father is perfect.

Can we truly be perfect? What does perfect mean in this passage. God has high expectations from us. Yet He is compassionate. What a Savior!

The Lord our God is merciful and forgiving, even though we have rebelled against him. Daniel 9:9a.

The apple of the eye is the pupil. It has been said that our eyes are the windows to our soul. We protect our eyes because of their importance to us. When the Ophthalmologist checks our eyes, he doesn't just glance into your eyes. No, he carefully looks inside the eye to see that all is as it should be. If you have ever had an eyelash or bit of dust in your eye, it is a constant irritation until removed. We protect our eyes. We wear sunglasses to keep the dangerous rays from damaging our eyes. As we so protect our eyes, the Lord protects us.

We are to search the Word of God carefully, reading over and over, taking apart phrases, looking for key ideas, carefully, and asking the Lord to teach us from it. When I was a little girl my daddy always called me the "apple of his eye." I was his only daughter. He felt not only deep love for me, but he also had a desire and responsibility to protect me. He was very protective about his children and I imagine he told my brothers the same thing.

For dad, being the apple of his eye meant that I would, in turn, value and respect that position in his heart. When I disappointed him, his heart would break. Dad often wrote letters and poems to express his feelings. He was a beautiful writer and his penmanship the same. As I was cleaning out some papers recently, I rediscovered this poem, written when I came in late one night. I don't know how late I was that night, but for dad, five minutes past 11 was late! Beside my bed that night, was this poem that is now about 50 years old:

To my Precious Daughter

To mom and me you're very dear
So sometimes we kind of live in fear
To you my darling, we may seem stern
It is because we have concern
We don't want you to think we're mean
Because our love for you is so keen.

Please understand us darling one
Sure we want you to have fun
That's what young people always do
That's what we want for you
Don't forget honey you're our only girl
That's why sometimes we're in a whirl

I as your dad am very proud
Of you my dear in any crowd
You're the apple of my eye
Then when you're late I sit and sigh
Not because I think you're bad
Indeed not, that would be sad.

Honey, when you have problems come to me
Let's look them over and you'll see
That I shall try to understand
With all the love I can command,
To do for you what I think best,
We'll put each problem to the test.

Love, Dad

That may not be proper or great poetry, but to me it is very precious. Dad knew that he would accomplish more with a letter I would read and re-read than if he had shown his anger to me or raised his voice to me. In fact, here it is for me to read again 50 years later. God has sent his love letter to us as well, to teach us wisdom, to guide us, to discipline us. He also wants our love and respect. Love includes respect for authority and submission to God and to my earthly father as well as to my Heavenly Father.

Various dictionaries tell us that the "apple of your eye" is one you highly treasure or love the most. Most likely you have either been called the apples of someone's eye or told someone they were the apples of your eye.

Can you remember a time when you were called the apple of someone's eye, or a similar endearing term? How did that make you feel?

Take time to tell those you love how you feel about them.

Tell your Heavenly Father how you feel about Him as well.

Things God has taught me in prayer...

LESSON TWO
Listen Up

When you receive a phone call from your family or dear friend, you recognize their voice right away. You know that voice because you are well-acquainted with the person who belongs to the voice. You can usually tell from the opening "Hello" how that person is doing, if all is well or if there is something troubling them. When your loved ones phone you, or come in the door and greet you, your heart rejoices to hear their voice.

When we read God's Word, when we study and spend time in worship and prayer, we become better acquainted with the Lord. His Word becomes precious, we long to spend time learning from it. When we spend time in prayer, we begin to commune with our Father in heaven. As we bow in the throne room of God, and are quiet before Him, He can begin to speak to us through the Holy Spirit who teaches us. We start to recognize His voice as we do that of our family and dear friends.

My sheep listen to my voice; I know them, and they follow me. I give them eternal life, and they shall never perish; no one can snatch them out of my hand. ~ John 10:27

This lesson truly comes from my heart to yours. One of the most persistent lessons the Lord has had to teach me is to listen to Him, to trust His perfect will when I think I know better, and to follow with all my heart.

God's waiting room is a difficult place to be at times. When we are concerned for a child, when we have sought the Lord and pleaded with Him for them, He often makes us wait. Our part is to be faithful, to never stop praying, to trust and obey.

When friends are in trouble or ill, we bring them before the Lord in prayer, sometimes day after day and even hour after hour. He promises to listen to our prayers, He has time for each of us and desires that we come to Him in praise, petition and thankfulness. We are told in Philippians 4 to be thankful in all circumstances. There are some circumstances that are very difficult to feel thankful for at the time. Yet, we are told to be thankful in all situations. This is one of the hard doctrines to understand, except that we know that God is good. Sometimes it is much later when we see that good.

Read Philippians 4. Choose three verbs from the chapter that speak to your heart, or to your need. Write them below.

1. _____
2. _____
3. _____

The blessings are great when you obey the Word of the Lord. His joy will fill your heart. You will learn the Word.

But in your hearts set apart Christ as Lord. Always be prepared to give an answer to everyone who asks you to give the reason for the hope that you have. – I Peter 3:15

List three benefits for understanding God's Word, and being able to express your beliefs in a clear and understandable way.

1. _____
2. _____
3. _____

The Lord wants us to be prepared by knowing His Word. Spending time in the Bible each day and time in prayer will prepare your heart when someone asks you why you have hope or joy. You will be eager to share because you know the source of your hope.

Open a hymnal and read the words to: Lord, Speak to Me

Apples of Gold was a true calling to my heart from the Lord. I was in a listening mode because I was at a crossroads in my life. I did not want to follow my own path, but follow His. Proverbs 3:5-6 tells us that when we trust Him with all our heart, He will do just that.

I was not asking God for a ministry. I wasn't seeking one. I just asked Him "what, Lord, shall I do with this thing called retirement? What plan do you have for me at this point in time?"

His answer to me was clear, succinct, exciting and sure. I knew without a doubt that He planted the thoughts in my heart and was asking me to obey. It was the first time in my life when I heard His voice so clearly. I knew it was HIS voice.

It was so moving and exciting that it remains a distinct and clear memory to me every time I recall it.

After that mountaintop experience, listening became an urgent call for me. I was used to going to God with my assessed needs, desires and thoughts, and seeking His approval. Listening to Him changed all of that. I now realize that listening to Him and obeying Him is the path to true joy and peace.

When God called me to start *Apples of Gold,* my entire life changed. I was asked to do things I was sure I could not do, but I had such a deep trust that God was standing right with me, and that gave me a new courage.

At that time, we were studying Moses in our Island Bible Study in Florida. I remember Moses' attitude when God told him to speak. Moses argued with God until God became angry with him.

"Who made your mouth?" God inquired of Moses.

Have you ever argued with the Lord? It is like telling God that we know what is best for us, right?

During my time of arguing with God, He gave me a song, which I call The Journey.

> I'm the Lord your God, come and follow me
> From your bondage of sin I will set you free
> With a pillar of cloud and a pillar of fire
> I will never tire, come and follow me.
>
> When you cannot walk, I will carry you
> When you cannot speak, I will speak through you
> On roads rocky and steep and through valleys deep
> I will ever keep, I will carry you.
>
> I will praise you Lord for you set me free
> When on Calvary's cross you died for me
> Took my burden of sin, gave me peace within
> I will praise you Lord for you set me free.
>
> And through all my days I will follow you
> Till I reach heaven's home I will follow you
> When by redeeming grace, I will see your face
> And forever more, I will give you praise.
>
> *Copyright Betty Huizenga 2000*

That song is my testimony. God has set me free from the bondage of my sin and leads me by his Spirit. He has carried me through deep waters. He has given me peace in troubled times. And I do want to be faithful to Him until I see Him face to face. Oh, what a day that will be!

Have you ever thought you heard the voice of God speaking to you through the Holy Spirit to your heart? What did He tell you or ask of you? Did you obey?

Quiet your heart and listen right now. What is God speaking into your heart today?

Things God has taught me in prayer...

LESSON THREE
Learning to Hear God's Whisper

*In a desert land he found him, in a barren and howling waste. He shielded him and cared for him, he guarded him as the **apple of his eye**. Deut. 32:10*

Read about Elijah's desert experience. Can you see how the Lord's revelation to Elijah, showed His great love and protection for Him?

I Kings 19:9-13

After being threatened by Jezebel, Elijah fled to the desert. Frightened and defeated he sat under the broom tree and prayed that he might die, then fell asleep. An angel came to him twice and brought him food. He continued 40 days and nights to Horeb where he went into a cave to spend the night.

The Lord came to him and said, "Go out and stand on the mountain in the presence of the Lord, for the Lord is about to pass by."

Then a great and powerful wind tore the mountains apart and shattered the rocks before the Lord, but the Lord was not in the wind.

After the wind there was an earthquake, but the Lord was not in the earthquake. After the earthquake came a fire, but the Lord was not in the fire. And after the fire came a GENTLE WHISPER.

When Elijah heard it, he pulled his cloak over his face and went out and stood at the mouth of the cave.

When you hear the whisper of God, it is so powerful. Elijah covered his face. When God spoke to me on the mountains of West Virginia, calling me to start Apples of Gold, I wept with joy. Never before had I known so clearly that God was speaking this message just to me. It was not for anyone else to hear. It was my own call from God.

What does it take to hear the still, small voice of God amidst the clamor, noise and confusion of the world? It takes closeness to the Lord, sensitivity to the Holy Spirit and a deep desire to obey His voice.

Why did I hear the Lord so clearly that day? Certainly, He had tried to speak to me before. I believe it was because I was truly seeking Him, and believed He would answer my cries to Him.

Seek the Lord while he may be found; call on him whle he is near. Isaiah 55:6

Look in your concordance for other verses about seeking God. Write one of them below that speaks to your heart today.

What can you do to quiet the noise of the world and listen to the quiet of God? List three positive steps you can take.

1. _____
2. _____
3. _____

The topic of listening to God is not "fluffy stuff". No, LISTENING is a powerful learning tool that will give you a closer walk with the Lord.

We love to hear nice things about God ...GOD LOVES YOU, GOD IS GENTLE AND LOVING, GOD IS YOUR BEST FRIEND. All of those statements are true, but the Lord God is so much more. He is not only a loving God, but He is Holy, Righteous and Just, and He desires truth in our inward parts ~ our hearts and minds.

Surely you desire truth in the inner parts; you teach me wisdom in the inmost place. Cleanse me with hyssop, and I will be clean; wash me, and I will be whiter than snow. Psalm 51:6-7

Two years ago we had an enormous snowstorm around Christmas in Michigan. The snow was so deep, so glistening and white, it was irresistible. We just had to go out and play in it. We made snow angels and took photos sitting on our summer chairs piled high with snow. The snow was so white that it hurt our eyes. We needed sunglasses to play in the snow. Jesus Christ washes our sins away and makes us as white and glistening as that snow in His eyes. How Amazing!

The world has such a jaded view of who God is because there are many "spiritual" teachers passing on believable thoughts, ideas, even lies, to many who have never been taught absolute truth.

Read the story of Samuel's call from God in I Samuel 3.

    Why didn't Samuel recognize the voice of God at first?

Listening to God is a learning experience. As we practice listening in our daily devotional time, we will soon begin to hear God's whispers to our heart. What Joy!

Why is it so important to learn to listen to God?
    Because He is our Father in Heaven and He loves you.

Why is it important for your child to listen to you?
    It is because you love your children and want to teach them how to live a life that is purposeful, joyful, rich, loving and responsible.

We say, "Listen to mommy? This is very important. I want to teach you something. Look at me, look right into my eyes!"

Sometimes, perhaps often, your child may ask WHY? Your reply may be, "because mommy says so, or because mommy knows what is best for you, or mama doesn't want you to be hurt, or mama wants you to make better choices and decision.

SOMETIMES WE SAY, **Just Because!**

God has the right to tell us to listen, "Just because" as well.

Why is it important to listen to our husband, our friends, our own parents? It is because we all learn from one another.

Give an example of something you learned by listening to:
    Your spouse
    Your friend
    Your parents

Have you ever wanted to have a conversation with someone about something you consider important, and got, "uh huh" for a response? We know that someone is not really listening. Perhaps that "uh huh" comes from behind the newspaper. Perhaps you are the one who is not responsive. Change that!

GOD NEVER JUST SAYS "UH HUH" when we talk to him.

I have not always listened well to the Lord. I was an independent, "I can do it myself, kind of kid." CAN ANYONE RELATE TO THAT?

In Florida, we have lots of bugs and lots of exterminators. One of the companies, Truly Nolen, advertises with their vehicles. My very favorite is a VW bug with mouse ears and a long black tail.

One day I sat at the stop light behind one of these adorable creature cars. When it started down the road, I followed it and I noticed something amazing. The faster the car went, the more the ears flopped back. As I watched that little car with amusement and laughter, the Lord spoke directly into my heart.

"Betty, that is just like you. The faster you go, the more things you do, the more trouble you have listening to me." I still smile when I see those cars because they are a constant reminder to me…, "Betty, Listen to me, I want to protect you because I love you as the apple of my eye."

As delightful as that little reminder is to me, there were other disasters in my life that came from my independent, disobedient heart. The night before our fourth child was born, we moved into a brand new home. Every day we had been painting and working to finish on time. But babies don't wait, and with paint still on the top of my legs, which I could not see too well enough to scrub off, I went into the hospital to deliver. My painted legs were amusing to my husband and doctor though I was embarrassed and humiliated!

We came home to our busy family of four children, five and under. Life was grand, but the house was just too white for this lover of color. I had been told by my beloved, "no more painting for a while". Our budget was tight and we were exhausted. I nodded my assent, and looked at my white walls day after day for about seven months. Then I could no longer look. I needed color

I shall not quickly forget the day Lee left town for a couple days, giving me the perfect time to disobey him and, of course the Lord as well. I wanted the nursery to be a lovely blue. After all, you cannot put a baby in an all white room. How boring for her day after day to look at those bleak white walls. She would never thrive and be happy!

I purchased the paint knowing I could easily paint the room in one day and when my sweet husband saw it, he would just be so very pleased with the color...right?

I began painting with the entire gallon of paint on the top of the ladder. FIRST BIG MISTAKE.
    Paint only in small cans.

              SECOND BIG MISTAKE.
                  Paint when small children are napping.

No sooner had I begun than our fast crawling son invaded the bedroom, shook me on the ladder, laughing with glee and dumping the paint bucket. It splattered as it hit the hardwood floors, putting large globs of paint on the walls, and landing on his baby sister's little head which she immediately began smearing in her hair as she screamed. Mark crawled out of the room as fast as he could, dragging the wet paint with him over the floor and onto the carpet in the hall. I began crying…no sobbing. Grabbing the children and heading for the bathroom, I heard the door open in the kitchen. It was my parents. Praise God for understanding parents! And for God's timing! He extended much undeserved grace to me that day.

My parents began scrubbing children and scraping as much paint as possible from all the places it landed. There was no good answer. The paint was everywhere! Even when we moved out a few years later, there were telltale signs of blue paint.

As I painted my dining room blue recently, some 40 years later, I was reminded once again of that story. You know, I didn't tell Lee this time either. He was in Alaska on a fishing trip. But this time was different. I had not been forbidden, and I knew he would be delighted, because he had agreed to help me paint it. What a difference truthfulness and honor make in a relationship. God expects the same!

There are some things I have learned living life and by listening to others:
1. When we love Jesus, it shows. Obedience shows we love Jesus.
2. My parents were more precious to me than I often deserved.
3. Being with friends and family who love me encourages my heart.
4. Having a child or grandchild fall asleep in your arms is a glorious thing.
5. Kindness shown and kindness received is a great blessing.
6. Friends are a treasure from the Lord to keep me on track and make me laugh.

7. Faith talks I had with my dad as a teenager have deeply affected my life
8. Abolishing a strict bedtime on occasion to lie down with my family under a full moon creates memories for a lifetime.
9. Being thankful God gives me what He knows I need rather than what I think I need.
10. It is important to surround myself with people of wisdom.
11. Bitterness and an unforgiving heart can make you sick.
12. A smile can change an entire day.
13. Knowing that God loves our children more than I ever could comforts me when I worry about them.

List several things you have learned by listening to God and others.

_____
_____
_____
_____
_____

Can you remember a time when you did not listen or obey? What were the consequences?

_____
_____
_____

Why am I so interested in this concept of learning to listen to God?

Because I have seen what one single experience of listening and obeying has meant in my life and that I don't want it to ever end…and I want my friends to experiencing it too!

THE OVERIDING PHRASE IN THE LETTERS I RECEIVE ABOUT APPLES OF GOLD IS : "THANK YOU FOR LISTENING TO GOD, OR FOR OBEYING GOD. It has made such a difference in my life."

We learn so much in life by listening. If I don't learn to listen, I will not know how to obey.

The way of a fool seems right to him, but a wise man (or woman) listens to advice. PROVERBS 12:15

What is the best advice you have ever received? How did it change your life?

_____

_____

_____

_____

Obeying the Lord is very important to me, because being outside of the will of God has often brought me pain and sadness. It is just a miserable place to be, isn't it?

Can you think of a time you refused to listen to good advice? What happened?

_____

_____

_____

_____

Obeying the Lord will bring peace even in the troubling times, because at least I am in His will for me.

Keep my commands and you will live, guard my teachings as the apple of your eye. Proverbs 7:2

Like the servant Samuel, I want to say, "Speak Lord, for your servant hears."

I WANT TO BE SO FINE TUNED TO GOD'S VOICE, THAT I CAN HEAR HIS WHISPER. IF HE NEEDS TO SHOUT AT ME, I AM IN A DANGEROUS PLACE.

Do you prefer a shout or a whisper in your ear? What a foolish question. When someone shouts at me, I am devastated!

FINE TUNING IS LIKE CLEAR CHANNEL RADIO OR TV. IT MAKES ALL THE DIFFERENCE IN THE MESSAGE WE RECEIVE.

Sometimes God uses people to speak His truth to us. I simply need to learn to listen.

God used two couples in our lives to lead us to Christ. Oh, how thankful we are that they obeyed God and shared with us. Even more thankful we are to have listened to them as they shared Christ with us. Those are true friends.

Sometimes God has used me to speak His truth to others.
- By inviting someone to dinner at His prompting
- By starting a neighborhood Bible study in our home
- By talking with someone I knew was ready to walk into a sinful trap.

And, of course, by listening on the mountains of West Virginia to His call to start APPLES OF GOLD.

Who does the Lord want you to listen to today? How does He want to use you to help someone else to listen? Will you do it?

Things God has taught me in prayer...

LESSON FOUR
A Heart Issue

Delighting in the Lord. Psalm 37:4-6

Delight yourself in the Lord and he will give you the desires of your heart. Commit your way to the Lord; trust in him and he will do this: He will make your righteousness shine like the dawn, the justice of your cause like the noonday sun. BE STILL BEFORE THE LORD and WAIT PATIENTLY for him.

Those verses contain promises. Did you claim the promises given? God's promises are true. He is all truth!

What are the desires of your heart? God knows the needs, the true desires of our hearts, and it is all about Him!

Matthew 6:19 says this:
Do not store up for yourselves treasures on earth, where moth and rust destroy and where thieves break in and steal. But store up for yourselves treasures in heaven, where moth and rust do not destroy and where thieves do not break in and steal. For where your treasure is there your heart will be also.

What are the treasures of your heart? BE HONEST

1. _____
2. _____
3. _____

Our treasures determine our heart attitude.

One of the songs we sing is, Lord, You are more precious than silver, Lord, you are more costly than gold. Lord, you are more beautiful than diamonds, and NOTHING I desire compares with you.

There are days when I choke on those words. Is there really NOTHING I desire as much as Jesus? Those words come right out of Proverbs.

Choose my instruction instead of silver, knowledge rather than choice gold, for wisdom is more precious than rubies, and nothing you desire can compare with her. Proverb 8:10-11

Lee and I talk often about the fact that everything we have is God's. He is good at reminding me that it is not ours, and that if God decides we don't need it, that is okay.

When Charley the Hurricane tore through Sanibel, Florida, that faith was put to the test. Was our Sanibel house really the Lord's or would we cling to it? I am amazed at the peace we had about that, the absolute realization that this was not up to us. We were in Michigan just watching the news. One day Geraldo Rivera was doing a report. At that time, we didn't know if we even had a house. As we watched the television intently we noticed our house right behind the head of Geraldo. What a gift from God! We just thanked and praised Him right there in front of the television.

Is it wrong to enjoy our homes and other blessings from the Lord? *He gives us all things richly to enjoy.* I Timothy 6:17b. Our homes are a gift from His hand. BUT REMEMBER THE ADAGE FROM YOUR YOUTH – SHARE!! There is joy and satisfaction in sharing our homes and possessions with others. Be looking for ways to share your home and heart with others who need refreshment.

James 1:17 tells us:
Every good and perfect gift is from above, coming down from the Father of the heavenly lights, who does not change like shifting shadows.

"We enjoy those gifts as long as they do not own us".

Our goal must be to have a heart that seeks after God. He is to be the primary treasure of our heart.

Matthew 6:33 tells us how to find that treasure. It is my husband's life verse.
"But seek first the kingdom of God and His righteousness, and all these things will be added unto you."

What things?
Perfect Peace
Perfect Love
Perfect Joy...
EVERY PERFECT GIFT

Jesus cares so much for us and He wants us to know that He is able to care for our needs, ALL OUR NEEDS. Not trusting Him by worrying is a lack of faith in His power and love.

The treasures you hide in your heart are not hidden FROM God. So hide your treasures carefully, making sure that whatever God sees in your heart is pure and precious to Him as well. He will surely bless you.

What did Paul write in Ephesians 1:18-19?
I pray also that the eyes of your heart may be enlightened in order that you may know the hope to which he has called you, the riches of his glorious inheritance in the saints, and his incomparably great power for us who believe.

Perhaps you are familiar with the contemporary chorus that is so popular today, "Open The Eyes Of My Heart Lord." If you know it, sing it to the Lord. There are others, "Open my Eyes that I may see," or "Open My Eyes, Lord, I Want To See Jesus." Pick a favorite and sing it several times today as a reminder to be looking for the wonder of God all around you.

WHAT DOES GOD WANT YOU TO SEE WITH NEW EYES TODAY? ASK HIM! DO IT!

When we prioritize our treasures, when our goal is to seek God first, we will more easily hear His voice when He speaks to us.

What things in your life may be interfering with putting God first?
_____
_____
_____

Ask the Lord to forgive you when you put other things ahead of Him, and seek Him first.

Things God has taught me in prayer...

_____
_____
_____
_____
_____
_____
_____
_____
_____
_____
_____

PART TWO: Results and Benefits of Listening to God

LESSON FIVE
Communion in God's Word

A DEEPER UNDERSTANDING OF THE WORD OF GOD AND COMMUNION WITH HIM.

How sweet are your words to my taste, sweeter than honey to my mouth! I gain understanding from your precepts; therefore I hate every wrong path. Your word is a lamp to my feet and a light for my path. Psalm 119:103-105

Honey is intensely sweet, a small amount goes a long way.

Our son-in-law is a beekeeper. It is a fascinating hobby. There are so many wonderful varieties of honey because each area has its own flowers and fragrances. Orange blossom honey tastes different from clover honey. There is not anything quite so wonderful as honey on toast!

GOD DESIRES that His Word brings sweetness to our lips. If God's sweetness is on our lips, our words to others will be sweeter as well. As honey lingers on the lips, the Word of God lingers in our heart!

The clues and treasures of our hearts are found in the Bible. We are to hunt for the clues and those 'nuggets of gold' in His Word and tuck them into our hearts and into the hearts of our husbands and kids.

Have you ever watched someone panning for gold?

It is fascinating. With just a small screen, the seekers search carefully for any sign of gold among all the silt that is gathered in the sieve.

That is how we are to search the scriptures. Take a small section, read it, then read it again. Ask three things:
> What does it say?
> What does it mean?
> What does it mean to me?

Take the very familiar John 3:16 and ask yourself those three questions.

For God so loved the world, that He gave His one and only Son, that whoever believes in Him shall not perish but have eternal life.

When a verse or portion of scripture really speaks to your heart, type it out, place it in a highly visible place in your kitchen or bathroom and memorize it. It will then be in your heart forever, just as your favorite hymns and songs are there even from childhood.

One night a few years ago, my husband and I were driving home over the Sanibel causeway. We were in our convertible and the moon was full. The night was just sensational with the full moon, the stars, the Milky Way. We were just in awe of God's creation and His gift to us that night.

I was reminded of a Psalm I had learned in grade school, Psalm 8. I began to recite it to Lee. He remembered learning it as well and together we recited the entire Psalm as we traveled those miles toward our home. It was just one of those "treasured moments" we will never forget. MEMORIZE. You never know when the recall of a text will carry you through a test or trial, or just give you great pleasure in the Creator of all.

Psalm 8

O Lord, our Lord,
How majestic is your name in all the earth!
You have set your glory above the heavens,

From the lips of children and infants you have
ordained praise because of your enemies,
to silence the foe and the avenger.

When I consider your heavens, the work of your fingers,
The moon and the stars, which you have set in place,
What is man (who am I) that you are mindful of him,
the son of man that you care for him?

You made him a little lower than the heavenly beings
And crowned him with glory and honor.

You made him ruler over the works of your hands;
You put everything under his feet;
All flocks and herds,
And the beasts of the field,
The birds of the air,
And the fish of the sea,
All that swim in the paths of the seas.

O Lord, our Lord,
How majestic is your name in all the earth!

The importance of learning scripture truths is not only for encouragement of our hearts BUT that our hearts may not be deceived.

See to it that no one takes you captive through hollow and deceptive philosophy, which depends on human tradition and the basic principles of this world rather than on Christ. Colossians 2:8

Our world is full of deceitful promises and ideas. We need to be able to recognize truth. Just look at television and magazine ads.

Recite a verse and hymn or chorus that is in your memory bank. What verse and song did you choose? Why do you think that verse and song came back to your mind and heart right away?

KNOWING THE WORD OF GOD WILL HELP YOU TO HEAR HIS VOICE WHEN HE SPEAKS. YOU WILL LEARN TO DECIPHER TRUTH. THE WORD IS POWERFUL.

If you spend time alone with God every day, His Word will protect you. We all know that this time with God is important, so I will not belabor it. It is a discipline that we all need.

JUST BE SURE TO GIVE GOD YOUR BEST TIME.

Things God has taught me in prayer...

_____

_____

_____

_____

_____

_____

_____

_____

_____

_____

_____

_____

LESSON SIX
Spending Time in God's Throne Room

Spending time in the presence of God in prayer will also teach you to be sensitive to His voice.

Before you start to pray, read Psalm 66:18

If I had cherished sin in my heart, the Lord would not have listened.

This is a most important verse. It does not say that if you sin or have ever sinned, God will not listen. It is talking about cherishing, holding on to the sin in your heart. First, confess the sins in your heart to God and release them from your heart, then your heart is ready to pray to a Holy, Holy, Holy God.

IMAGINE with me the throne room of a palace.

I see the throne, perhaps overlaid with gold. A long red carpet runs the length of the throne room up to the throne. The throne is elevated several steps above the floor. The king sits in royal robes with attendants all around. A staff is in his hand. Royal colors of scarlet, purple and gold are everywhere.

This earthly king, splendid and powerful, may or may not admit you to the throne room. I am pretty sure I would be thrown out and told not to return.

CONTRAST THE DIFFERENCE~

In God's throne room, you are always welcome. It is more beautiful than any earthly throne room could ever be, its beauty cannot be described. The presence of the Almighty God is there! He not only welcomes you, but He is waiting for you. Imagine that!

He says, "Come to me, I will listen. I will help you." Start your time in the throne room with this poem:

THRONE ROOM

Into your throne room, Lord I'm coming
Humbly I bow before your throne
Seeking to know your grace and wisdom
Yielding my spirit to Your own.

Teach me to listen when you call me
Give me a heart that's warm and kind
Reaching outside my place of comfort
Helping the sick, the lame, the blind.

Teach me to love as you have loved me
May all my life reflect your grace
Your Holy Spirit's power within me
All earthly doubts and fears erase.

And when my life on earth is ended
Before your throne my knee shall bow
I want to hear, "well done, my servant
Enter my heavenly kingdom now."

– Betty Huizenga

CREATE YOUR OWN POEM OR WRITING TO GOD ABOUT YOUR TIME WITH HIM.

Have you ever thought about how amazing it is that the Lord God is so accessible?

Remember the first time you held out your arms to a child and they responded to you by holding out their little arms to you?

God holds His arms open to you in the same way. He is eager for you to come to Him. We are safe with Jesus.

I Peter 5:7, Cast all your anxiety on Him, for He cares for you.

Look in your hymn book for a song about casting your care on Christ, or draw one from your memory. Sing it to the Lord with joy!

Even though the Lord is eager to have you come into His throne room, be sure to show the respect due the King of Kings. Don't just barge in. Come humbly. Come boldly, but come reverently.

Be sure to praise Him. One way to praise Him is by reading a Psalm of praise, such as Psalm 8 or Psalm 100.

My friend, Cathy, sent this e-mail to me:

Psalm 23:
   The Lord is my shepherd – that's relationship
   I shall not want – that's supply
   He makes me to lie down in green pastures – that's rest
   He leads me beside still waters – that's refreshment
   He restores my soul – that's healing
   He leads me in the paths of righteousness –
   that's guidance
   For His names sake – that's purpose
   Yea, though I walk through the valley of the shadow of death – that's testing
   I will fear no evil – that's protection
   For thou art with me – that's faithfulness
   Thy rod and staff comfort me – that's discipline
   You prepare a table before me in the presence of mine enemies – that's hope
   You anoint my head with oil – that's consecration
   My cup runs over – that's abundance

Surely goodness and mercy shall follow me all the days of my life – that's blessing
And I will dwell in the house of the Lord forever – that's eternity.

AS YOU READ A PHRASE FROM THE BIBLE, YOU CAN PUT IT INTO YOUR OWN WORDS OF PRAISE. YOU CAN PRAY YOUR WAY THROUGH A PSALM OR CHAPTER OF THE BIBLE. BY THE WAY, THIS IS A GREAT WAY TO TEACH YOUR CHILDREN TO PRAY.

Our closing lesson will lead us through a time of worship, study and prayer.

Things God has taught me in prayer...

LESSON SEVEN
A Mind That Seeks Wisdom

There are some days when I think I have lost my mind. I cannot remember why I walked into a room, I cannot remember a good friend's name, or where I left my glasses! Perhaps you have been there as well. This is happening more as I get older. Sometimes it takes two of us to put together a memory.

One way to keep our mind sharp is to study, to read, to memorize. Read verses several times. The first time, perhaps just skim it, then read it again carefully. Then read it looking for the verbs and important phrases. Write those down. It will help you to remember what you read.

The Lord created our mind and He desires that we acquire wisdom.

> *The proverbs of Solomon, son of David, King of Israel*
> *For attaining wisdom and discipline;*
> *For understanding words of insight*
> *For acquiring a disciplined and prudent life*
> *Doing what is right and just and fair*
> *For giving prudence to the simple*
> *Knowledge and discretions to the young*
> *Let the wise listen and add to their learning*
> *And let the discerning get guidance*
>
> *The fear of the Lord is the beginning of knowledge, but fools despise wisdom and discipline. Proverbs 1:1-7*

Verse 4 says giving prudence to the simple. The dictionary says prudence is common sense. God wants us to have common sense so that we make good decisions that will help us in our everyday lives.

A simple man believes anything, but a prudent man gives thought to his steps. Proverbs 14:15

Have you ever believed a story without checking it only to find out later that it was not true? Have you told a story that you heard without checking it? What was the result? What is prudence?

My mom was a great mom. She was really quick and smart, yet at times she made our day with her common sense bloopers… like the day she swallowed her diamond studs, or the day she took the phone off the hook to keep the line open. Mom's gracious spirit allowed her to laugh at herself and endeared her to us and to others. Her unselfish heart and love for others made her beloved to so many. What a precious woman!

Teaching common sense to your children is invaluable and will help them to make good choices in tough times.

Proverbs was written by Solomon, the wisest king. But even this wisest of kings was reminded by his own father, King David, in I Chronicles 28:9;

And you, my son Solomon, acknowledge the God of your father and serve him with whole-hearted devotion and with a WILLING MIND, for the Lord searches every heart and understands every motive behind the thoughts.

A willing mind indicates we have a choice:

If any of you lacks wisdom, he should ask God, who gives generously to all without finding fault, and it will be given to him. But when he asks, he must believe and not doubt, because he who doubts is like a wave of the sea, blown and tossed by the wind. That man should not think he will receive anything from the Lord; he is a double-minded man, unstable in all he does. James 1:5-7

Write three things God is telling you in this passage:

1. _____

2. _____

3. _____

I HAVE HEARD CHRISTIANS LIKE THOSE DESCRIBED IN THIS PASSAGE AS WINDSHIELD WIPER CHRISTIANS. They vacillate back and forth in their beliefs and ideas. God gives a stern warning for that kind of thinking.

What issues of life cause you to change your position back and forth from one thought or idea to another?

_____

_____

_____

Proverbs 1:9 and chapter 3:22 tell us that listening to wise instruction from our parents is a gift of life for us, like a garland of grace about our neck. It is like a visible blessing.

Wisdom is supreme; therefore get wisdom. Though it cost all you have, get understanding. Esteem her, and she will exalt you; embrace her, and she will honor you; Embrace her, and she will honor you. She will set a garland of grace on your head and present you with a crown of splendor. Proverbs 4:7-9

If you are a crafter, create a garland of grace from small flowers placed on a wire circle like a tiara. If you have children, they can help. Make it beautiful and place it where you will be reminded of its meaning for your life.

Over and over, Proverbs emphasizes the importance of gaining wisdom. Chapter two tells us the moral benefits of wisdom, that if we search for it as WE WOULD FOR A TREASURE, wisdom will be a protection for us.

On Sanibel Island, some of the great treasures are the beautiful and coveted sea shells. It is a common sight to watch the shell collectors doing the "Sanibel Stoop" as they bend over collecting these gifts from the sea. Finding a Junonia shell is cause for celebration and having your photo in the local newspaper.

Oh, if we would search for scripture treasures in the same way, stooping over the Word to find God's best treasures for our heart.

Verse 7-8 say that God holds victory for the upright. He is a shield for those whose walk is blameless, he guards us and protects us.

Come, O Zion! Escape, you who live in the Daughter of Babylon! For this is what the Lord Almighty says: "After he has honored me and has sent me against the nations that have plundered you- for whoever touches you touches the apple of his eye- I will surely raise my hand against them so that their slaves will plunder them. Then you will know that the Lord Almighty has sent me. Zechariah 2:7-9.

God is saying, "Don't mess with what is mine."

Do you long for God's protection for your life and for the lives of your loved ones? If you can teach children to make wise choices early on, if they learn to make their decisions based on the Bible, they will be so far ahead spiritually.

The same is true for us. It is never too late to seek the wisdom of God.

PRETTY IMPRESSIVE STUFF, WOULDN'T YOU SAY?

In what area of your life do you need the wisdom of God today? Just ASK.

Things God has taught me in prayer...

LESSON EIGHT
A Gentle Spirit

Listening to God with a sensitive heart softens our spirit and makes us more attractive to those we love and strangers alike.

I Peter 3 teaches us that inner beauty is more important than outward beauty.

"it should be that of your inner self, the unfading beauty of a gentle and quiet spirit, which is of great worth in God's sight."
I Peter 3:4

WE NEVER TIRE OF A GENTLE PERSON.

Philippians 4:5 says, *"Let your gentleness be evident to all."*

The fruits of the Spirit listed in Galatians 5:22 are:

> LOVE
>   JOY
>   PEACE
>   PATIENCE
>   KINDNESS
>   FAITHFULNESS
>   GENTLENESS
>   SELF-CONTROL

Each of these attributes comes from a pure heart, one that seeks after and listens to God.

List the fruits of the Spirit you believe you exhibit well. Then list the ones that need changing and growth.

_____

_____

_____

_____

_____

A GENTLE SPIRIT PRODUCES GENTLER WORDS AS WELL.

Do your words ever get you into trouble?

Out of the overflow of the heart the mouth speaks. Matthew 12:34

Everything we say reveals our heart.

Words kill; words give life. They're either poison or fruit; you choose. Proverbs 18:21

God really understands us, doesn't He? Sometimes it just feels like an eruption. Those words just flow out on someone, usually someone we really love, and then there is incredible hurt. Words like, "You are such a (you fill in the blank)," or "You always do such and such."

Words spoken in anger are hard to retract. They can be forgiven, but they can stick in the mind of the other person and they hurt. The well-known phrase, "think before you speak" is a worthy one.

Has anyone ever poured out their venom on you? It is devastating, isn't it? That overflow is like toothpaste, easy to squeeze out and impossible to put back in.

Someone has said, "The tongue weighs practically nothing, but few can hold it."

How many words would you take back if you could? Word to parents, spouses, children, a good friend, even to a stranger?

Have you slandered anyone with your words lately?
Have you attacked someone's character or reputation?
Have you gossiped?

In as much as it is possible, make those things right with the person you have hurt. Such cleansing is necessary and returns joy to our spirit.

"If it is possible, as far as it depends on you, live at peace with everyone." Romans 12:18

My dear brothers, take note of this: *Everyone should be quick to listen, slow to speak and slow to become angry. For man's anger does not bring about the righteous life that God desires. Therefore, get rid of all moral filth and the evil that is so prevalent and humbly accept the word planted in you, which can save you. James 1:19*

What are the words you long to hear?
     I love you
     I am praying for you
     I forgive you
     Can you come to dinner Friday night?
     You're the best mom!

        KIND WORDS MAKE GOOD ECHOES

Things God has taught me in prayer...

LESSON NINE
A Peaceful Heart

A peaceful heart comes from listening to God

Zephaniah 3:17 is one of my favorite verses:

The Lord your God is with you, He is mighty to save, He will quiet you with His love, He will rejoice over you with singing.

What an amazing thought! What comfort! What joy! Can you imagine the Lord singing over you? Such love the Father has bestowed on His children. Rejoice in Him!

God alone can truly quiet our hearts.

A peaceful heart means inner peace. How can we obtain that inner peace? Peace comes from an absolute surety that God is in control.

What are the attributes of God? Look them up in your study Bible or check your Concordance for words that describe God and only God. Write some of them below.

Understanding who God is, draws us closer to Him. Understanding, for instance, that a God who is completely Holy loves me...now that is amazing!

ATTRIBUTES OF GOD

Find as many attributes of God as you can in your Concordance. List them below and describe what they mean. For instance:

God is Holy, Holy, Holy
God is Omnipresent

_____

_____

_____

_____

_____

_____

_____

Now read Philippians 4 again and read verses 4-7

Rejoice in the Lord always. I will say it again; Rejoice! Let your gentleness be evident to all. The Lord is near. Do not be anxious about anything, but in everything by prayer and petition, with thanksgiving, present your requests to God. And the peace of God, which transcends all understanding, will guard your hearts and your minds in Christ Jesus.

We often start with DO not be anxious, but we need to start with "Rejoice in the Lord".

How can we rejoice in the midst of fear and worry? By understanding who is in control. We understand who is in control by understanding the Heavenly Father.

Next comes the verse we read just before.

Let your gentleness be evident to all. We just talked about developing a gentle heart.

How often have the stresses of life taken away your gentleness? What's the first thing that happens when we begin to worry?

We become agitated and frustrated. We are overcome with our problem and it is all consuming. Jesus teaches us to rejoice in Him, He will care for us, be calm.

Our gentleness in the midst of the storm is our testimony to the power of God.

Can you begin to see how all these heart issues are connected?

He quiets our souls in the midst of the storm. We do not have to wait for the storm to be over.

The next thing we are told in the Philippians 4 passage is "do not be anxious." Anxiety is deep worry. The word literally means "TO PRESS TIGHT", to strangle, to be weighed down with grief.

Have you ever experienced that kind of troubled heart?

There was a time in my life when I suffered panic attacks. No matter what others told me, I could not seem to get over it. I still have to talk to myself at times.

OUR WORRY is a poor testimony as a Christian. If we have no peace, our friends and family will not be attracted to Christ through us.

Oswald Chamber said, "God's children slander God by worry and anxiety."

Taste and see that the Lord is good. Blessed is the man who takes refuge in him.

Fear the Lord, you his saints, for those who fear him lack nothing.

The lions may grow weak and hungry, but those who seek the Lord lack no good thing.

COME MY CHILDREN, LISTEN TO ME; I WILL TEACH YOU THE FEAR OF THE LORD." Psalm 34:8-14

Jesus beckons us to fall into his arms with complete abandon, promising to hold us, to calm us, to secure our hearts.

The more we are filled with Jesus, the more we are filled with His peace. When we are filled with Jesus, there is less room for worry, doubt and fear...for Satan, if you will.

REMEMBER THE SLOGAN?
>No Jesus, No Peace
>Know Jesus, Know Peace

Satan is the great doubt-maker. He is a liar and deceiver. We must listen to the voice of God and that can only happen when we are in close fellowship with Him.

Satan flees when we praise God. So if you struggle with fear and worry, play Christian music in your home and car. AND VISIT THAT THRONE ROOM OFTEN.

In addition, we need to be a peacemaker. Be the one to establish peace in your home. If you set the example, others will follow.

Make every effort to keep the unity of the Spirit through the bond of peace. Ephesians 4:3

What are some of the things that prevent a peaceful heart?

Fear
>*For God did not give us a spirit of timidity, but a spirit of power, of love and of self-discipline. II Timothy 1:7*

Worry
>*Therefore I tell you, do not worry about your life, what you will eat or drink or about your body, what you will wear. Is not life more important than food, and the body more important than clothes? Matthew 6:25*

Anger
>*An angry man stirs up dissension. Proverbs 29:22*

Sing a song about God's peace to the Lord, such as:
- -I've Got Peace Like a River
- -It is Well With My Soul
- -Peace, Perfect Peace
- -Wonderful Peace

If you have trouble sleeping at night, pray and sing to Jesus in your heart. I hear from many of my friends who struggle to sleep at night. It is frustrating because we need sleep. When we are stressed and exhausted, our body shows it. A peaceful heart restores our health.

The thing that most keeps me from sleep is my busy mind. It wanders and imagines and things get bigger and scarier. In Isaiah 26:3 we read this:

You will keep in perfect peace him whose mind is steadfast, because he trusts in you.

The King James version uses "whose mind is stayed on thee". We must learn to focus our mind on Christ and remember His perfect love and protection for us.

I find those times of disquiet can be overcome by prayer, and by listening to God. So often He speaks to my heart in the night. Most songs and poems I have written have come to me at night. I believe my best writing has been done at night after the Holy Spirit has spoken in the quiet to my heart. IT IS AN ESPECIALLY REAL AND HONEST TIME.

When God speaks to my heart in the night, I find it helpful to write it down immediately. In the morning, it can be gone. Keep a pad and pencil beside your bed. Someone even gave me a pen and pad with a little light on it so I could see what I was writing.

At night I am actually quiet enough to listen.

I will lie down and sleep in peace, for you alone, O Lord, make me dwell in safety. Psalm 4:8. What a great verse to memorize and teach to your children.

If you are up with a child at night, pray over your child as you feed or comfort him. Sing to him praises to the Lord for him. It will comfort the child's heart and your own as well.

I always loved caring for our grandchildren. One of the best parts was rocking them, especially in the hammock and singing songs about Jesus to them. What a privilege! And what a reminder those simple children's songs are to my own heart.

He who fears the Lord has a secure fortress, and for his children it will be a refuge. Proverbs 14:26

Is your home a secure fortress, a refuge for your family? If not, how can you change it to make it that safe and secure place?

Just as your children feel safe in your arms during a storm, we are safe in the arms of Jesus during the storms of life. Rest in Him, wait patiently for Him, He is the giver of peace.

Things God has taught me in prayer...

_____

_____

_____

_____

_____

_____

_____

_____

_____

_____

_____

LESSON TEN
A Joyful Spirit

A spirit of joyfulness comes from knowing His will in our lives and being in a position of obedience.

We are talking about true joy, the kind that comes from deep inside. OF COURSE it doesn't hurt us to laugh a bit as well. IT IS SAID that a smile is a crooked line that helps set thing straight.

Our joy is often expressed in our face. That is a scriptural principle. My husband has a joyful countenance. He reflects Christ on his face.

A happy heart makes the face cheerful, but heartache crushes the spirit. Proverbs 15:13

May the righteous be glad and rejoice before God; may they be happy and joyful. Psalms 68:3

A cheerful look brings joy to the heart, and good news gives health to the bones. Proverbs 15:30

A cheerful heart is good medicine, but a crushed spirit dries up the bones. Proverbs 17:22

Doctors agree that laughter can be physically and emotionally therapeutic. So be sure to laugh at your house. Laughter helps diffuse those negative emotions we mentioned earlier: Depression, Anxiety, Fear and Anger.

Doctors have written, "Mirthful laughter is a total body activity that conditions the heart muscle, exercises the diaphragm, abdominal and thoracic muscles and improves lung activity." What a great way to exercise!

Do you laugh a lot in your home? Do you have time to listen to the best stories of the day from your family? And do your children see you laughing with your spouse and friends?

IT IS PART OF JOY

Listening to God helps erase those four negative emotions: fear, worry, depression and anxiety, which all come from the heart. They can keep you from fellowship with the Lord.

The joy of the Lord is our strength. Nehemiah 8:10

We need the joy of Jesus, not manufactured joy.

One of the things that can rob us of our joy is our perception of ourselves. Understanding who we are in the eyes of God can make a huge difference. Psalm 139 explains very clearly what God knows about us: That he is totally involved in our lives. He knows where I am, where I am going, what I am thinking, what I will say even before I say it, his hand is always on me and I can't escape His presence day and night. He is always with me.

He KNIT me together in my mother's womb and he never dropped a stitch.

I am a knitter. Our daughter owns a yarn shop. WE KNIT! WE are YARNIES! If you are a knitter, you understand that dropping just one stitch will ruin the entire garment unless it is repaired.

God gets it right the first time! When He created own son Mark, who was born with Downs Syndrome, He did not drop a stitch or make a mistake. Mark is just the right Mark for us. His life is not only a blessing to us, but to so many others as well.

You are precious to God, He cherishes you. Cherish means to hold dear, to treat with care and affection, to keep deeply in mind.

Do you feel cherished? If you are not feeling cherished in your heart today, know that you are cherished by God.

Being cherished by God gives great joy even in the darkest times. Knowing that God is intensely interested in you, while being just as interested in your family is an amazing and comforting thought. Ah, what bliss to know that I am His child and He loves me enough that He died for me.

How great is the love the Father has LAVISHED on us, that we should be called children of God! And that is what we are! I John 3:1

Lavish love is that over the top kind of love, overflowing and generous. It reminds me of whipping cream melting down over a hot fudge sundae.

Things God has taught me in prayer...

PART THREE: Quiet Time with God
Practicing the Presence of Jesus Daily

Apple of His Eye
Daily Time in the Throne Room

Have you been listening to the Lord?
Has He spoken to your heart?
Are you eager and willing to obey?

THERE ARE CONSEQUENCES TO DISOBEYING THE LORD. I PRAY THAT YOU WILL CHOOSE OBEDIENCE, and receive wisdom and understanding, a gentler spirit, immeasurable peace, and abundant joy.

The Lord has a rich plan for your life. It is revealed through His Holy Word, Through Prayer, and in Listening to His WHISPER.

COME, NOW IS THE TIME TO WORSHIP!

Some of you are very comfortable with long periods of prayer time, for others, it may be difficult even knowing how to start. I hope this outline will help you.

I pray that the Lord will fill you with wisdom and joy as you serve Him with joy and purpose.

Read again this promise from Zephaniah 3:17

> The Lord your God is with you
> He is might to save
> He will take great delight in you
> He will quiet you with his love
> He will rejoice over you with singing.

In your quiet time:
- Get settled
- Sing your favorite chorus or hymn to the Lord
- Read the following verses. After the first day, search the Word for your own choice of verses.

> Teach me your way, O Lord,
> And I will walk in your truth;
> Give me an undivided heart
> That I may fear your name.
> Psalms 86:11

> As water reflects a face
> So a man's heart reflects the man
> Proverbs 27:19

> You will find me when you seek me with all your heart
> Jeremiah 29:13

> For where your treasure is, there will your heart be also.
> Matthew 6:21

> For out of the overflow of the heart the mouth speaks
> Matthew 12:23

"MEDITATE"

TAKE TIME TO MEDITATE ON HIS ATTRIBUTES:
- His Holiness
- His Wisdom
- His Righteousness
- His Justice
- His Omniscience
    - (He knows everything)
- His Omnipresence
- His Faithfulness
- His Power
- His Unchanging Nature
- His Perfect Love

Praise Him for those things
Take time to meditate on who are you in the eyes of your Creator

What are YOUR attributes and gifts? List them and ask the Lord how He wants you to use them for Him:

1. _____
2. _____
3. _____

Take time to look at your heart
Examine your heart, thoughts and motives,
Confess all known sins to God, being transparent and honest

Remember one of God's attributes is that He knows everything. You can hide nothing from Him, but even though He already knows everything about you, He still wants to hear your confession.

THIS VERSE IS VERY IMPORTANT! THERE IS A CONDITION. HERE IT IS:

If I had cherished sin in my heart, the Lord would not have heard me. Psalms 66:18

Sin creates a barrier between God and man. Cherishing sin means holding on to the sin, being unwilling to surrender to the will of God. It does not mean that God will not listen to you because you have sinned. Repent and ask forgiveness for any known sinful thoughts, words or actions. Ask the Lord to reveal sins for which you are unaware. Open your arms in thankfulness for His generous forgiveness.

Ask the Holy Spirit to fill you, to teach you and to give you a sensitive and willing heart.

NOW, just be quiet before God and listen.
"Be still and know that I am God." Psalms 46:10

~ Don't try to tell God anything more.
~ Don't argue with Him.
~Write down every thought that comes into your mind, even the distracting thoughts, like how busy you are, or how silly this seems!

_____
_____
_____
_____
_____
_____

When you sense that this time of listening is finished,
   Look over your "thought" list and sort it.
How good were you at listening to God? Did the world get in the way? Learning to listen to God takes practice and diligence.
   Each time you spend this kind of time with God, you will be less distracted by the world and LONG to hear Him speaking to you, You will find yourself looking forward to this precious time each day.

WHAT DID YOU HEAR FROM THE LORD TODAY?
What do you think God is telling you?
Will you choose to obey?

THE END!

Epilogue:
Teaching Your Children to Worship

IN my little bed I lie, Heavenly Father, hear my cry. Lord, protect me through the night, wake me with the morning light. Bless mommy and daddy and my brothers, and grandpa and grandma...

That was my childhood prayer. It isn't a bad start for little ones, but there is so much more to teach our children about worship and prayer.

Fix these words of mine in your hearts and minds; tie them as symbols on your hands and bind them on your foreheads. Teach them to your children, talking about them when you sit at home and when you walk along the road, when you lie down and when you get up. Write them on the doorframes of your houses and on your gates, so that your days and the days of your children may be many in the land that the Lord swore to give your forefathers, as many as the days that the heavens are above the earth. Deuteronomy 11:18-21

This passage tells us that we are to teach our children about the Lord all the time, morning to night, during learning times throughout the day.

Perhaps you can also write them on the doorframes of your houses with scripture sayings to remind the children as they walk through the house, that this is God's house.

Over the window of our living room we have written this verse:
A heart at peace gives life to the body. Proverbs 14:30

Choose a family verse and write it somewhere in your home as a reminder of God's faithfulness and presence.

People were bringing little children to Jesus to have him touch them, but the disciples rebuked them. When Jesus saw this, he was indignant. He said to them, "Let the little children come to me, and do not hinder them, for the kingdom of God belongs to such as these." ...And he took the children in his arms, put his hands on them and blessed them. Mark 10:13-14 and 16.

Have a time that your family gathers to have family devotions. Let the children participate by reading the Bible, singing a song, or sharing something God has done in their lives. This prepares them to be "ready to give an answer" to their friends. Encourage your children to learn to pray aloud so they get used to hearing their voice in prayer. It is okay to start with a memorized prayer, but then encourage them to talk to the Lord with their own words. Then when someone asks them to pray, they are ready and confident.

Equally important is teaching your children to have their own quiet time with God. You can use the outline you use and modify it for them:
    Sing a song of praise
        Read a scripture
            Memorize a verse
                Teach them to talk to the Lord about everything
                AND MOSTLY,
    TEACH THEM HOW TO DISCERN THE STILL,
        SMALL VOICE OF GOD.

When a child learns to make this time a part of daily living when they are small, they will have it to carry them throughout their life.

        May the Lord bless you and keep you
        May the Lord make His face to shine on you
            and give you peace.